Are YOU Breathing?

Published in the United States of America
ISBN   Paperback: 978-1-959165-16-3
ISBN   eBook: 978-1-959165-17-0

ReadersMagnet, LLC
10620 Treena Street, Suite 230 | San Diego, California, 92131 USA
1.619. 354. 2643 | www.readersmagnet.com

Book design copyright © 2022 by ReadersMagnet, LLC. All rights reserved.

Cover design by Ericka Obando
Interior design by Dorothy Lee

Are YOU Breathing?

Gretchen Reininga-Yates
Illustrated by
Michael Ploog

ReadersMagnet, LLC

For Everyone
who Breathes

The Lord Blew into Adam's nostrils

THE BREATH OF LIFE,

and Adam became a living being.

Genesis 2:7

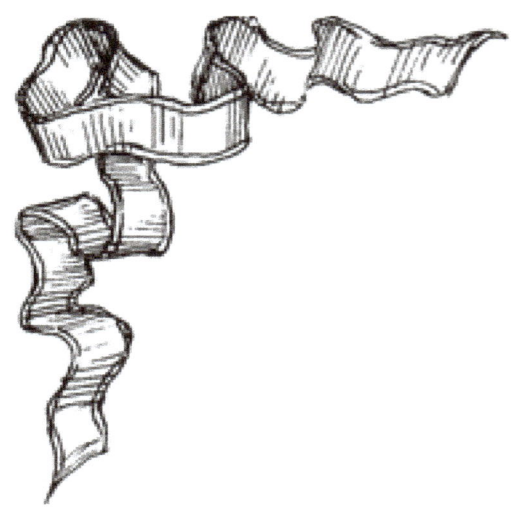

Are YOU Breathing?

Our World is filled with concerns and anxieties of mortgage loans, school achievements, relationships, economic concerns, national and world politics, new devastating diseases, effects of noise, and polluted crowded environments.

There is a place within us that I call

THE STUFFING PLACE.

It can grow and grow to finally become who we think we are; unresolved Rage, Anger and Fear of losing control.
A place of yesterdays and tomorrows.
A place of falsehood and fantasy.

ANXIOUS FOR EVERYTHING

This is the WARDOG – a painting by Michael Ploog.

This is what I call

the MUNCHIN'; CRUNCHIN'; SUCKIN'; ANXIETY RIDDEN STUFFIN' PLACE.

The REALM of YOUR Irrational Emotions

Rage, Anger & Fear.

Now, an up close and personal look at the
REALMS of YOUR

MUNCHIN'; CRUNCHIN'; SUCKIN'; ANXIETY RIDDEN STUFFIN' PLACE.

Are YOU Breathing?

The TONGUE

quivering for the craved.

What goes into your mouth

day in and day out

and SICK WITHOUT IT?

The TONGUE will not be denied

The *MOUTH*

opening wide,

with teeth sharp and vicious.

Spewing words

HARSH AND THOUGHTLESS

The MOUTH will not be denied

Controlled and timid

YOU stuff and stuff

YOUR emotions

with **Stuff!**

The TONGUE and MOUTH,

CRAVING day in and day out.

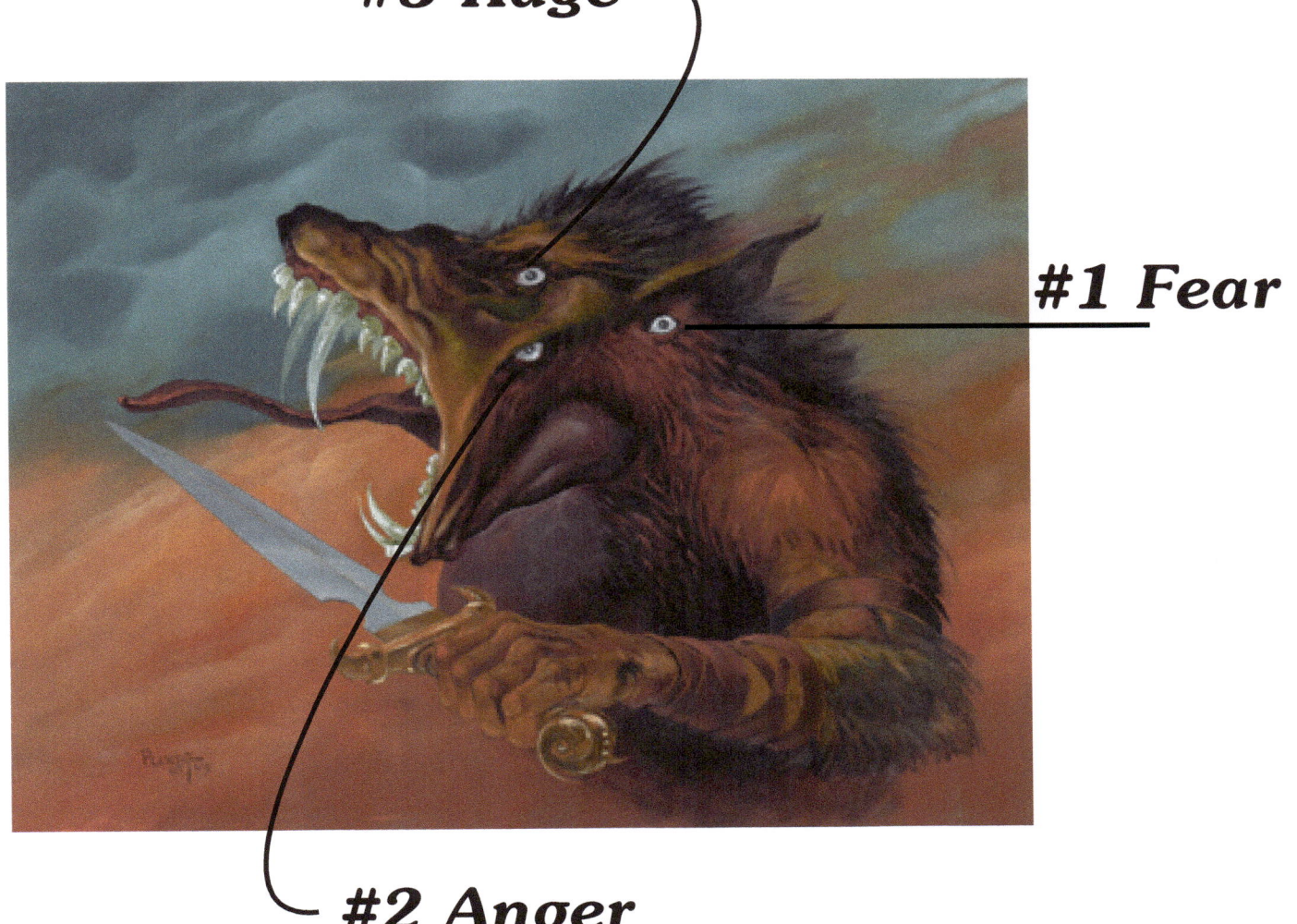

#3 Rage

#1 Fear

#2 Anger

The REALMS of Irrational Emotions.

The REALM of
Fear of Losing Control

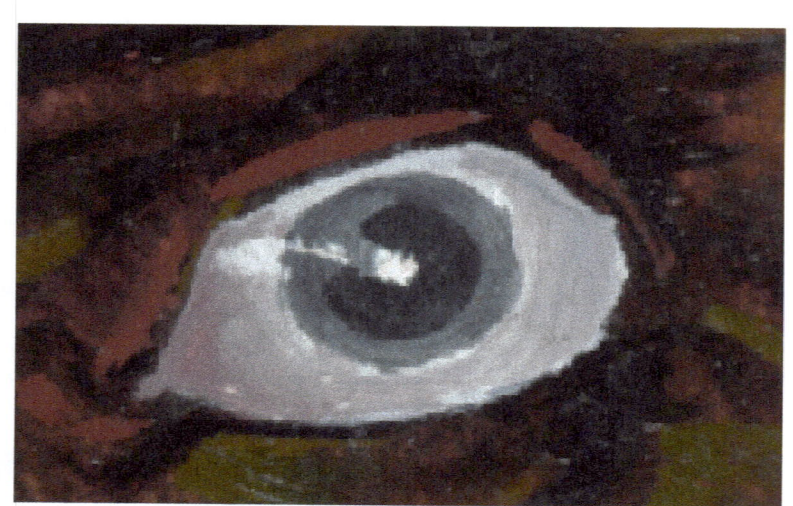

The Realm of
ANGER

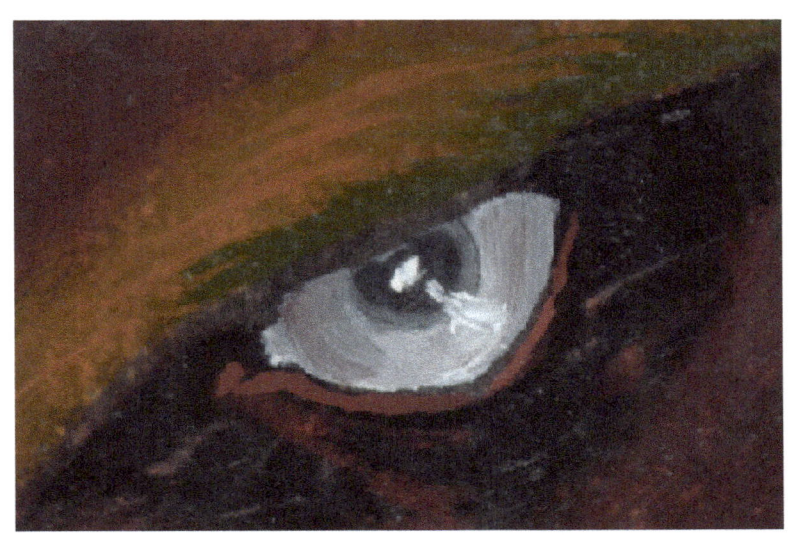

Turned on by FEAR of Losing Control

The Realm of
RAGE

Turned on by ANGER all Foul and Nasty

While in YOUR REALMS of Irrational Emotions

YOU have no time

YOU are always busy

YOU complain, dissatisfied and unhappy

YOU sulk in your despair

YOU have no fun

YOU do not laugh

YOUR mind is a racket

"Never mind, go away, leave me alone!"
a thin line marks the mouth

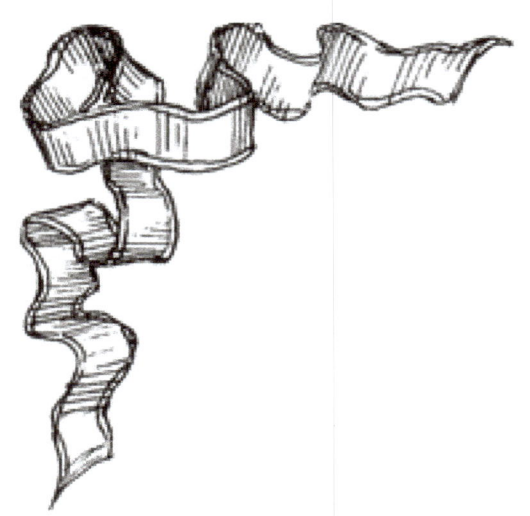

You are SAD,

so very SAD.

Feeling only

the MUNCHIN', CRUNCHIN', SUCKIN' ANXIETY RIDDEN

cravings coming on.

NOTHING *Good comes out of*

The MUNCHIN', CRUNCHIN', SUCKIN' ANXIETY RIDDEN STUFFIN' PLACE

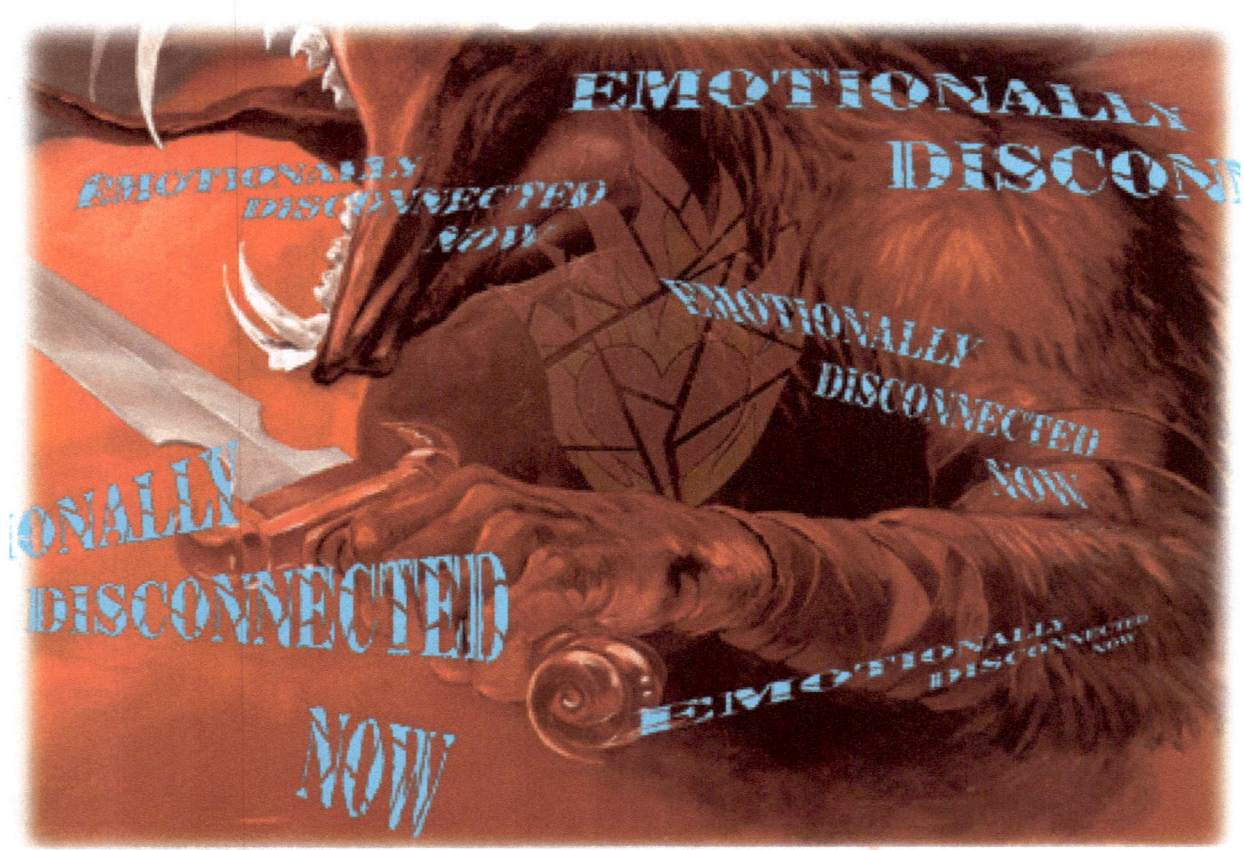

EMOTIONALLY DISCONNECTED

I saw the Lord always before me.

Because he is at my right hand, I will not be shaken.

THEREFORE my heart is glad and my tongue rejoices;

my body will also rest secure.

Psalm 16 v 8&9

THE JOURNEY

BEGINS WITH YOUR BREATH.

Breathing through your mouth filling the body like a balloon nice and easy letting the breath out naturally; not jerky or shallow, which keeps the **MUNCHIN'; CRUNCHIN'; SUCKIN'; ANXIETY RIDDEN STUFFIN' PLACE** *alive and ugly*

Now BREATHE over

**The QUIVERING TONGUE
and EXHALE**

BREATHE until the quivering craving stops.

DRINK SOME WATER

Your mind is a racket of thinking, craving something for....

THE MUNCHIN', CRUNCHIN', SUCKIN' ANXIETY RIDDEN STUFFIN' PLACE

Now BREATHE into the MOUTH

and EXHALE
TAKE YOUR TIME

Now *BREATHE into RAGE*

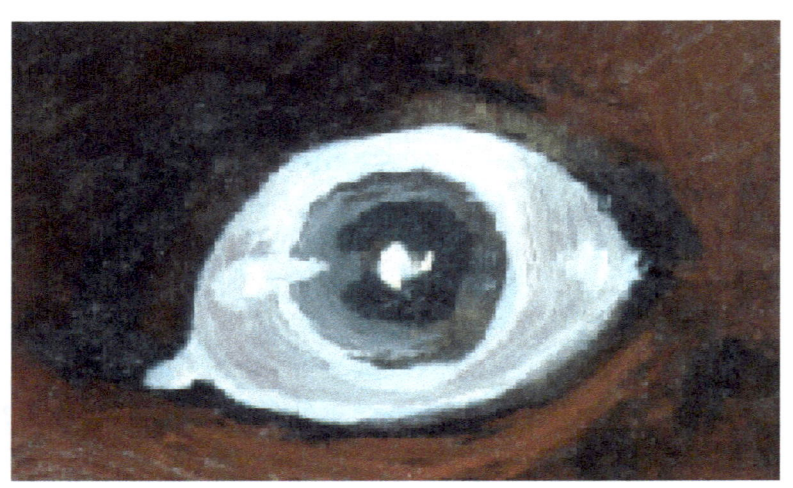

and *EXHALE*
TAKE YOUR TIME

*Now **BREATHE** into **ANGER***

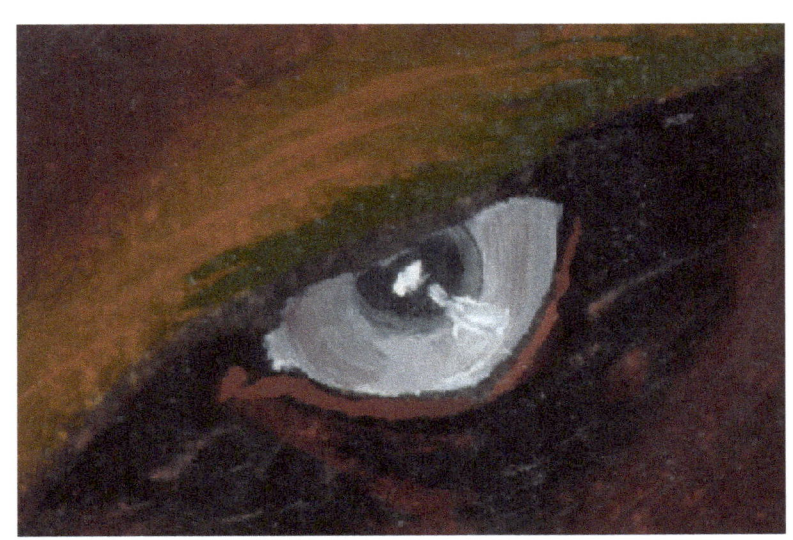

*and **EXHALE***
TAKE YOUR TIME

Now BREATHE into FEAR of Losing Control

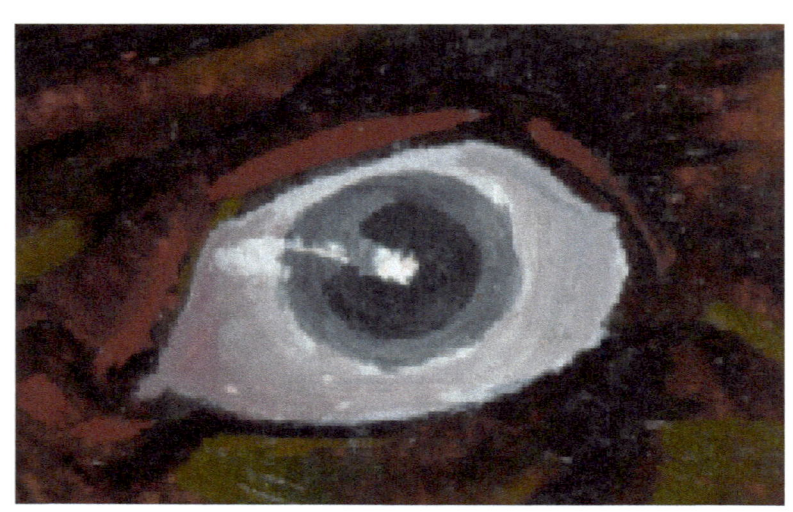

and EXHALE
TAKE YOUR TIME

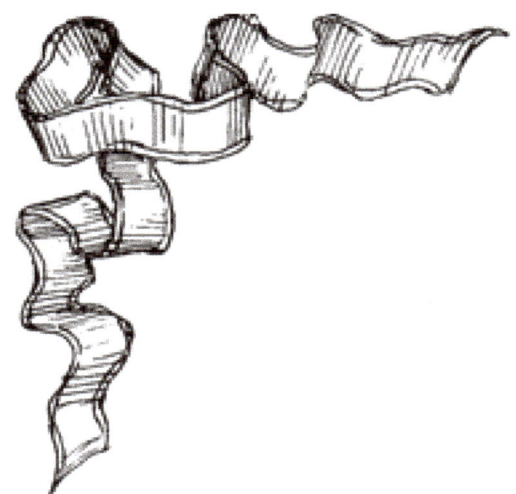

Are YOU Breathing?

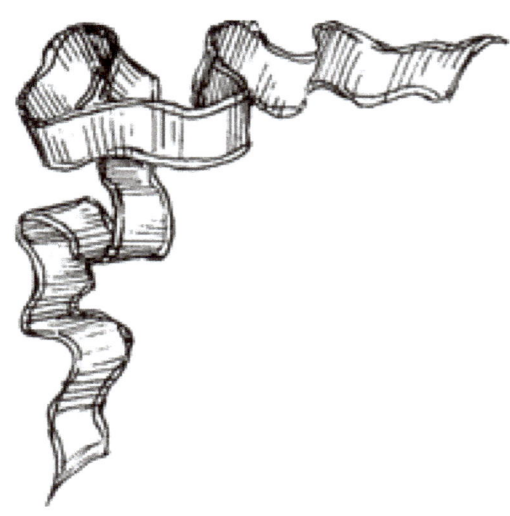

Brought you right back with YOUR BREATH, didn't I?

Enter YOUR SPIRIT

Who YOU are
YOUR AUTHENTIC SELF
YOUR PLACE OF INQUIRY & WATCHFULNESS

YOUR SPIRIT is the PLACE of trust, compassion, caring, warmth, respect and joy – without FEAR of losing control, ANGER and RAGE.

EMOTIONALLY CONNECTED NOW

ANXIOUS AGAIN?

Quick get back to the
QUIVERING CRAVING TONGUE.

Subdue it with your **BREATH,**
and
DRINK SOME WATER.

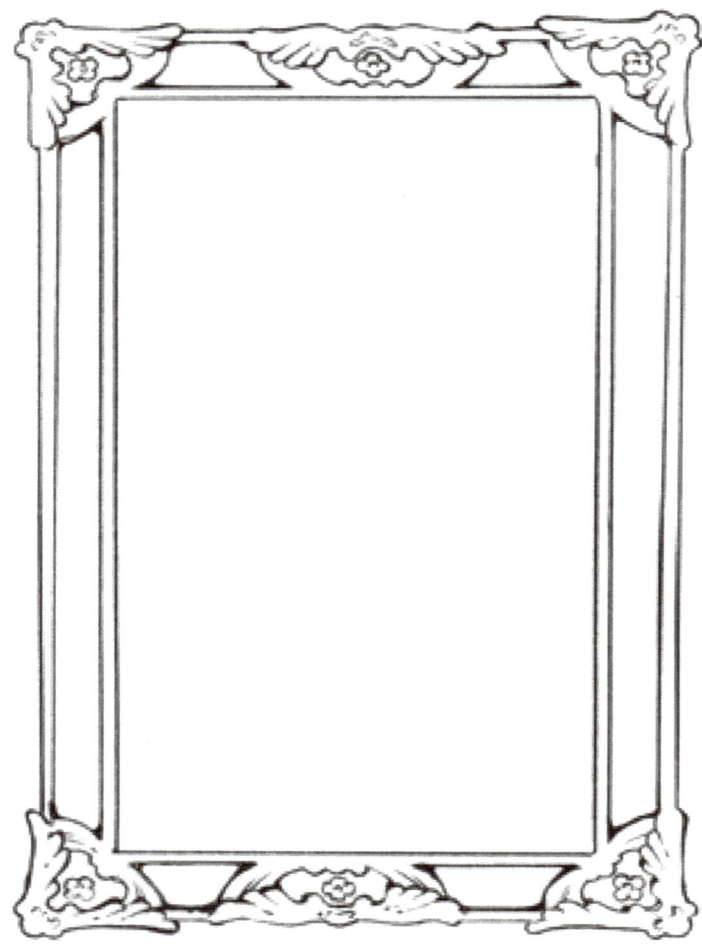

Are YOU Breathing?

Keep on BREATHING

over the QUIVERING CRAVING TONGUE again

**Keep on BREATHING
through YOUR MOUTH**

**with TEETH so sharp
and words so HARSH and THOUGHTLESS**

Keep on BREATHING

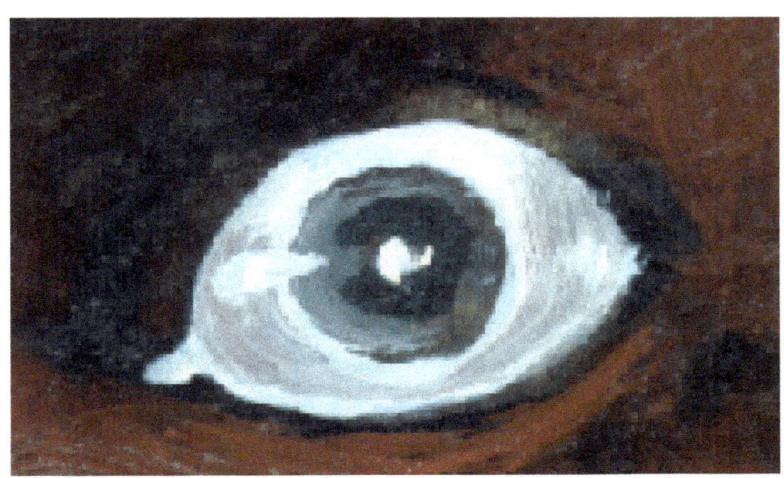

all the way back through RAGE

Keep on BREATHING

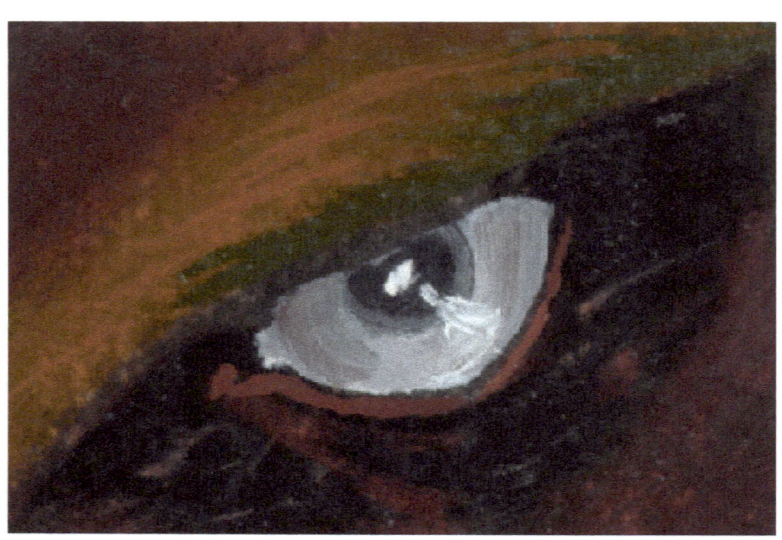

all the way back through ANGER

Keep on BREATHING

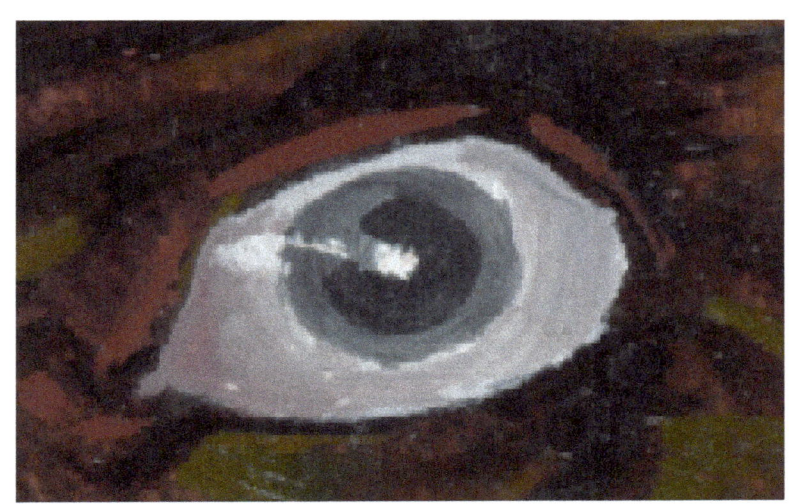

through YOUR FEAR of losing control

WHOA, WHAT'S THIS?!

Why it's the SNAG
For immediate gratification of YOUR

MUNCHIN', CRUNCHIN', SUCKIN'
ANXIETY RIDDEN STUFFIN' PLACE

Like a Breeze
BREATHE right past it

Say
bye bye SNAG
and
DRINK SOME WATER

KEEP ON BREATHING

TAKE YOUR TIME

Back into your SPIRIT

Who YOU are

Now again, BREATH through

**the MUNCHIN'; CRUNCHIN'; SUCKIN';
ANXIETY RIDDEN STUFFIN' PLACE.**

BREATHING

over
the QUIVERING CRAVING TONGUE
DRINK SOME WATER

BREATHING through YOUR MOUTH

and EXHALING
Take YOUR time

BREATHING back through YOUR RAGE

and EXHALING
Take YOUR time

BREATHING back through YOUR ANGER

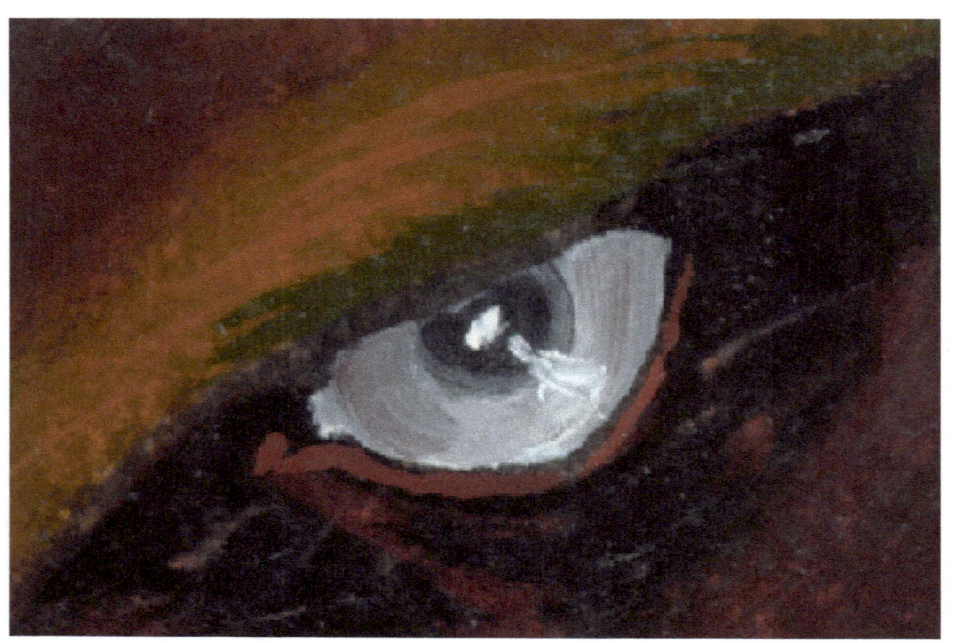

and EXHALING
Take YOUR time

BREATHING back through FEAR of losing control

and EXHALING
take YOUR time.

**Sometimes the pain in this REALM is hard to get through.
Just keep on BREATHING**

Past your SNAG
Of the MUNCHIN', CHRUNCHIN', SUCKIN',
ANXIETY RIDDEN STUFFIN' PLACE

bye bye SNAG

Drink some water

KEEP ON BREATHING

TAKE YOUR TIME

Back to YOUR SPIRIT

Who YOU are
THE REALM OF INQUIRY & WATCHFULNESS

YOUR SPIRIT, with your BREATH

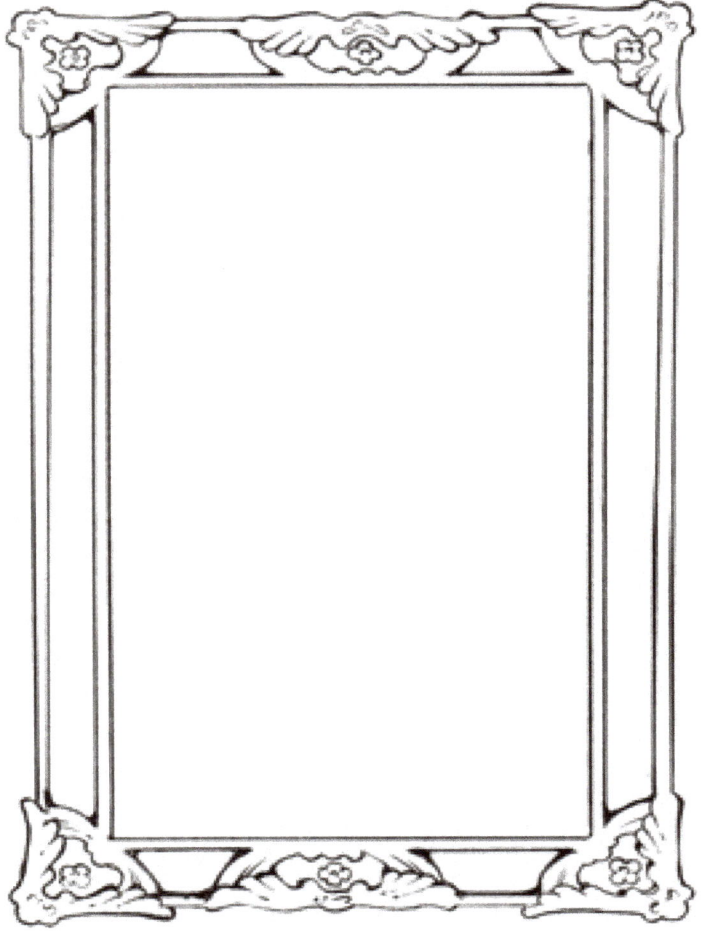

manages the MUNCHIN', CRUNCHIN', SUCKIN', ANXIETY RIDDEN STUFFIN' PLACE.

Every DAY

Every HOUR

Every MINUTE

Every SECOND

DAY IN AND DAY OUT

BREATHING

BREATHING
the MUNCHIN', CRUNCHIN', SUCKIN', ANXIETY RIDDEN STUFFIN' PLACE

OUT!

KEEP ON BREATHING

TAKE YOUR TIME

Keep on BREATHING

over YOUR QUIVERING CRAVING TONGUE

through YOUR MOUTH

**with TEETH so sharp
and words so HARSH and THOUGHTLESS**

Through your RAGE

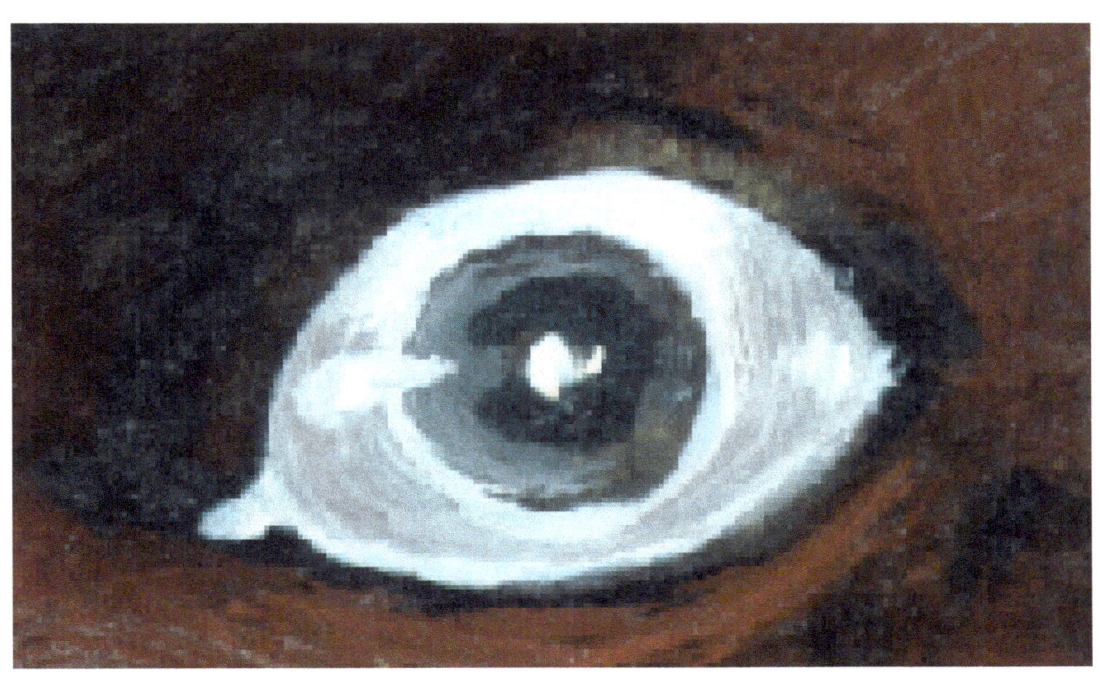

HEART RELAXING

through your ANGER

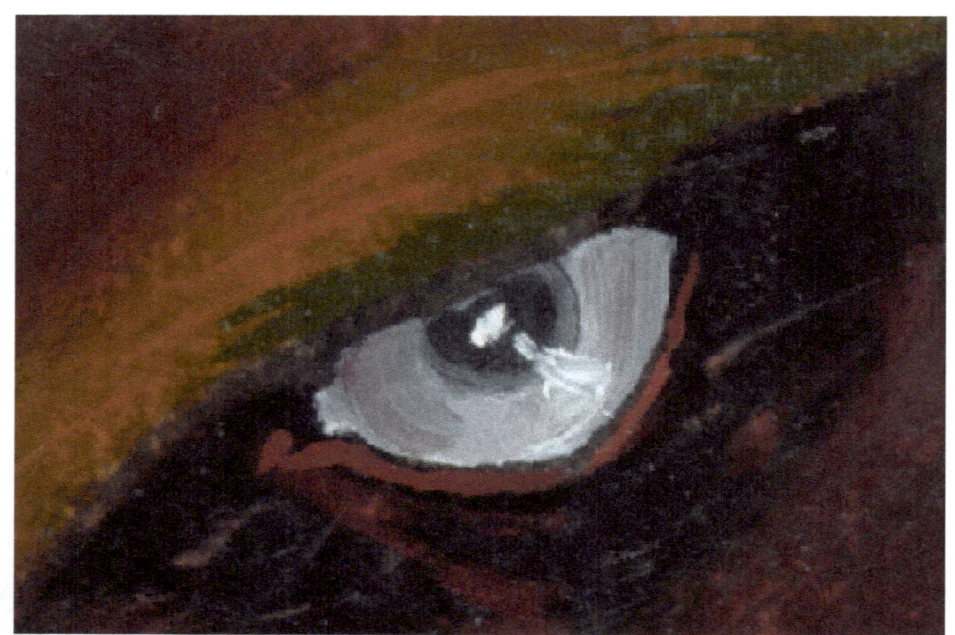

NECK AND SHOULDERS RELAXING

through YOUR FEAR of losing control

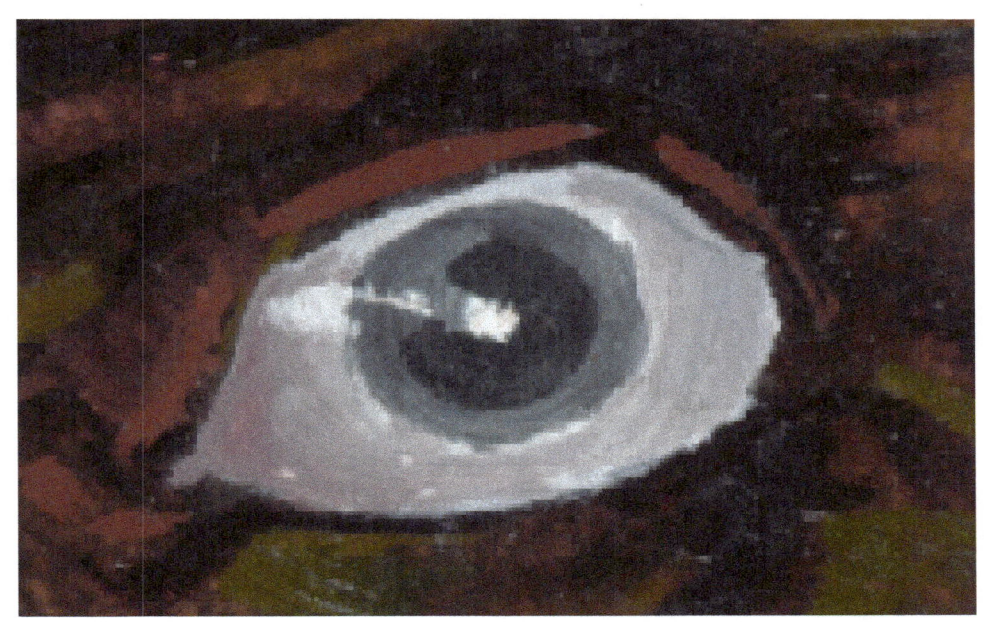

RACKET HAS STOPPED, MIND IS AT EASE.

Past your SNAG
For immediate gratification.

bye bye SNAG

Drink some water

KEEP ON BREATHING

TAKE YOUR TIME

And here YOU are again and again

**IN YOUR SPIRIT A BRIGHT CLEAR PLACE.
YOUR REALM OF INQUIRY & WATCHFULNESS.
YOUR "HEARING" GOD PLACE**

YOU listen,
Now YOU WILL hear.

YOU taste,
Now YOU WILL savor.

YOU look,
Now YOU WILL see.

YOU touch,
Now YOU WILL feel.

YOU breathe,
Now YOU WILL smell

"THE ROSES."

WAIT!

Who are YOU?

SPIRIT?

OR

THE MUNCHIN', CRUNCHIN', SUCKIN',

ANXIETY RIDDEN STUFFIN' PLACE?

Are YOU Breathing?

Go through the JOURNEY again.

BREATHING through your mouth
belly EXPANDING like a balloon
belly CONTRACTING as the breath is exhaled.

BREATHING over the TONGUE

QUIVERING AND CRAVING
Losing its grip
DRINK SOME WATER

BREATHING through the MOUTH

gone are the TEETH sharp and vicious
gone are the words harsh and thoughtless.
gone with the BREATH

BREATHING through RAGE

A nice big breath here in and out
Keep on BREATHING

BREATHING through ANGER,

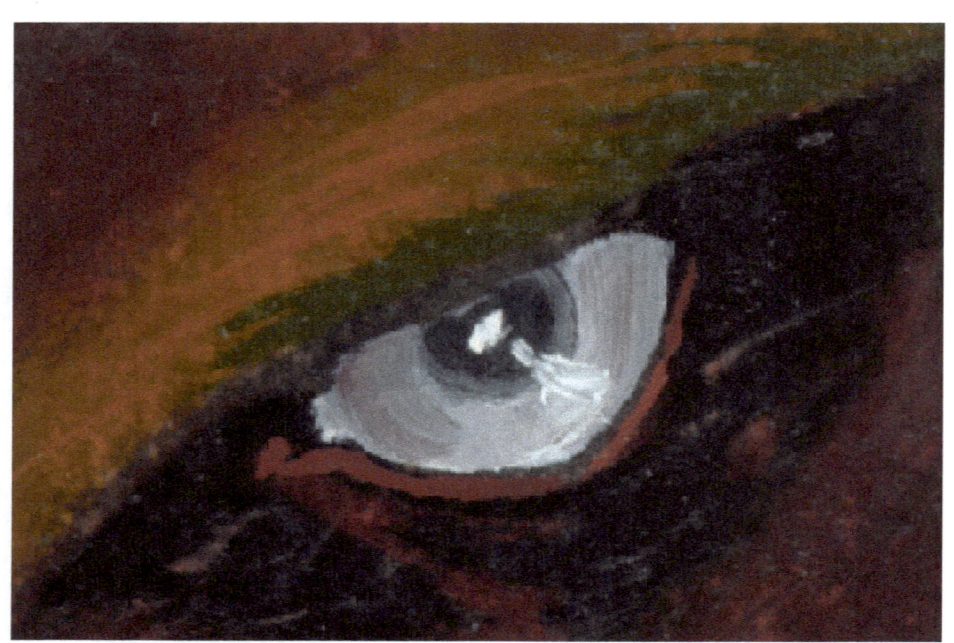

A sigh of relief!
Keep on BREATHING

Into FEAR of losing control,

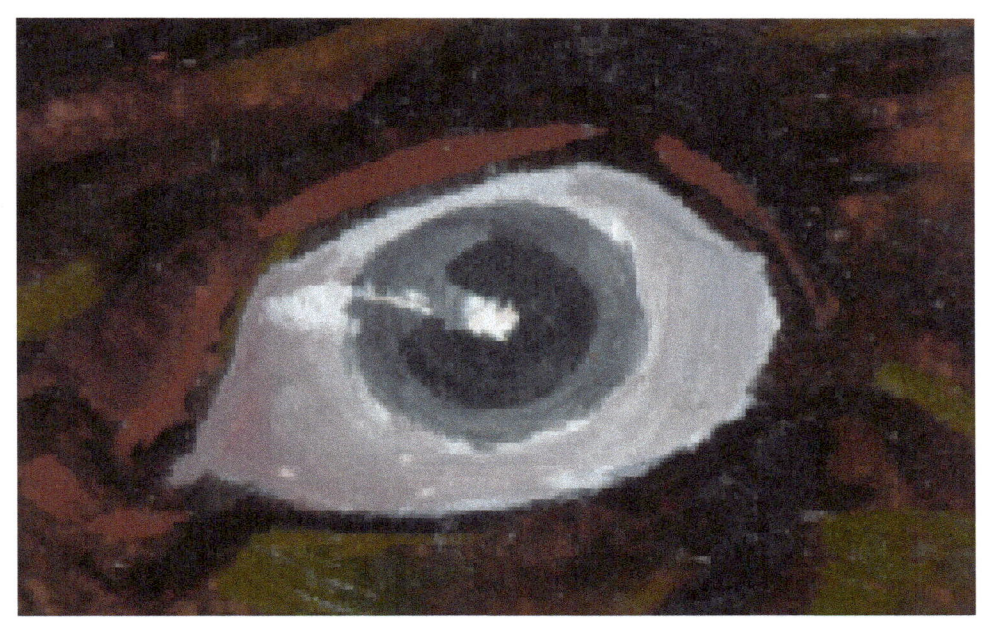

No pain now.
Keep on BREATHING

BREATHING back into your SPIRIT

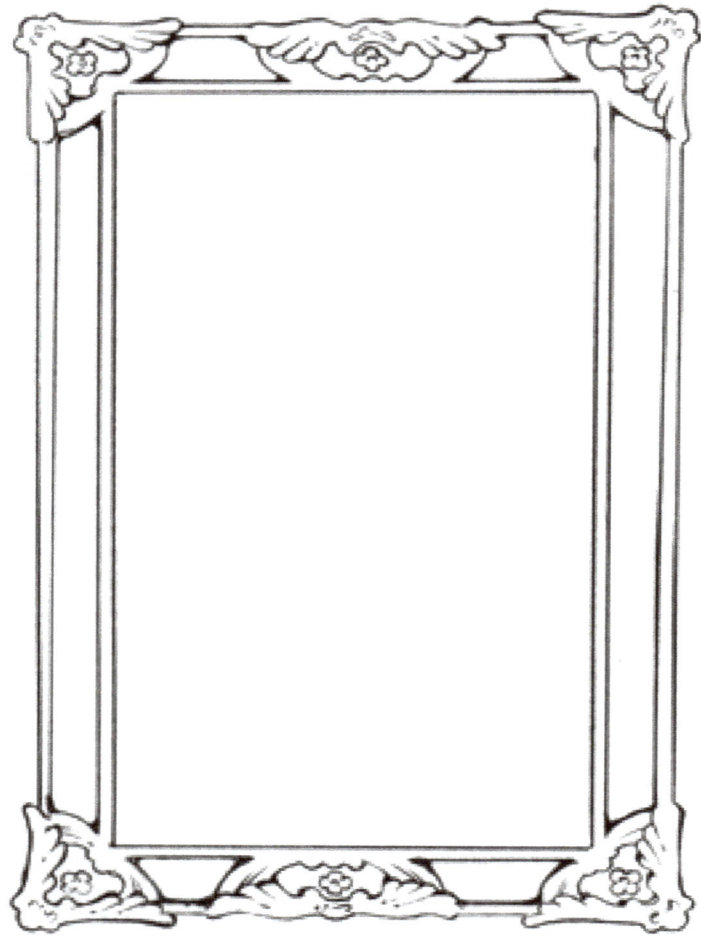

YOUR PLACE OF LOVE and FORGIVENESS.
It is here WE know WE were loved before WE loved.
It is here WE love our neighbor as OURSELVES.

YOUR FEER of losing control
Obliterated

YOUR ANGER
Banished

YOUR RAGE
Extinguished

YOUR CRAVINGS
Mitigated

Are YOU Breathing?

LAUGHING now in YOUR SPIRIT

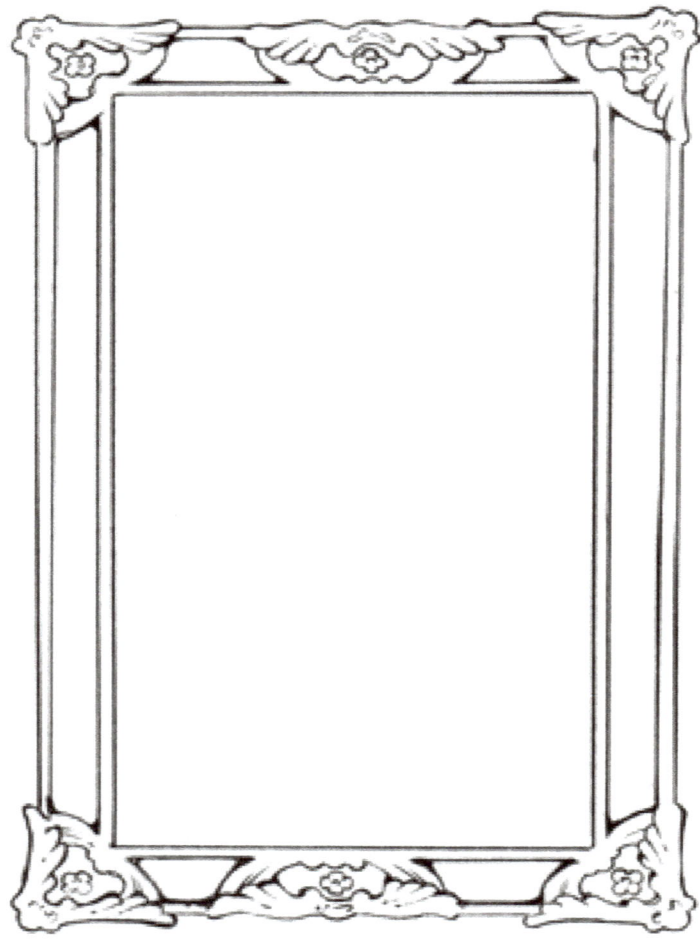

who YOU are,
that CLEAR BRIGHT PLACE
YOUR AUTHENTIC SELF.

You have made known to me the path of life;

You will fill me with joy in your presence…

Psalm 16 v 11

THIS IS
NOT
THE END

This is the BEGINNING

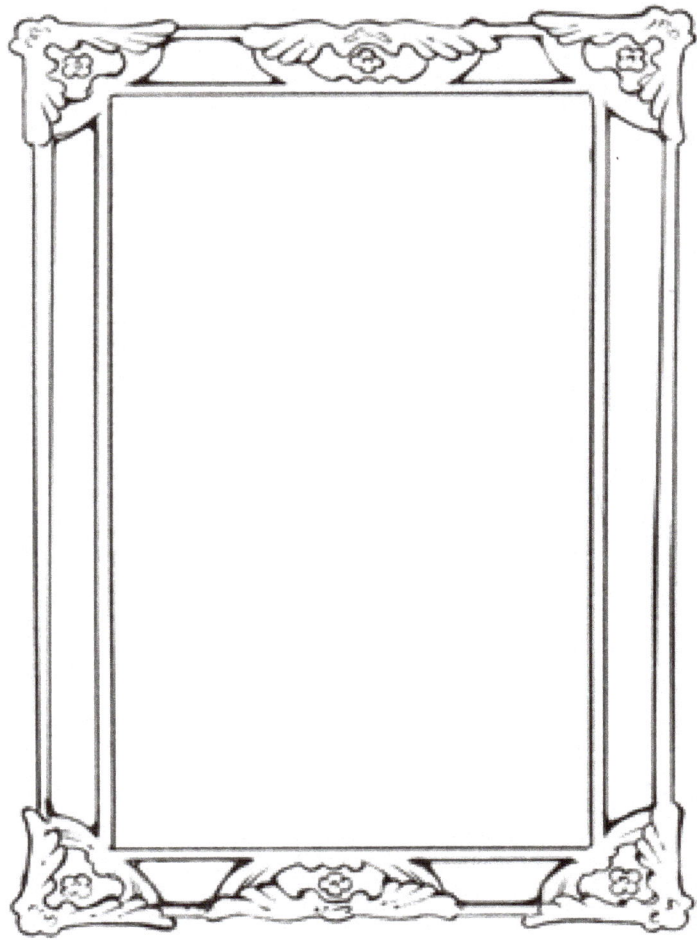

YOUR REALM of YOUR JOY
THE FRIENDSHIP of YOUR EMOTIONS and SPIRIT
ANXIOUS FOR NOTHING

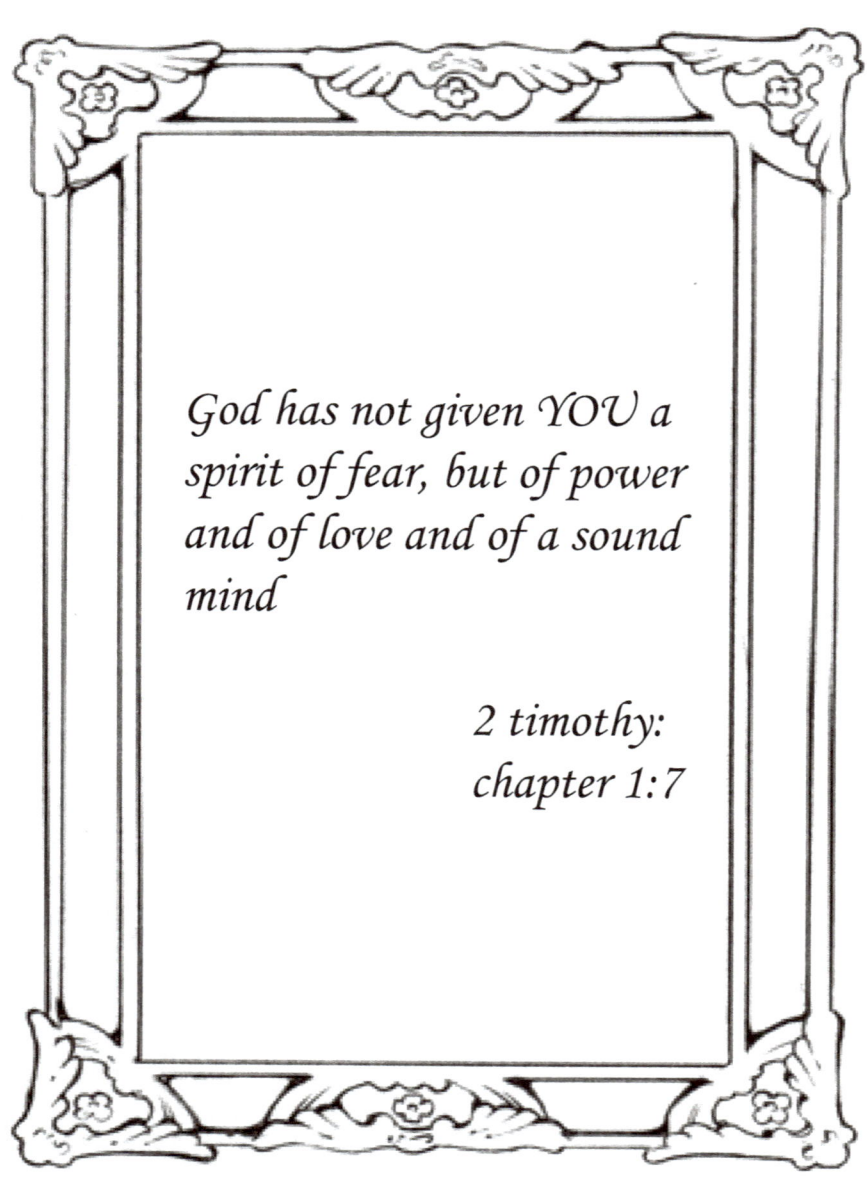

God has not given YOU a
spirit of fear, but of power
and of love and of a sound
mind

2 timothy:
chapter 1:7

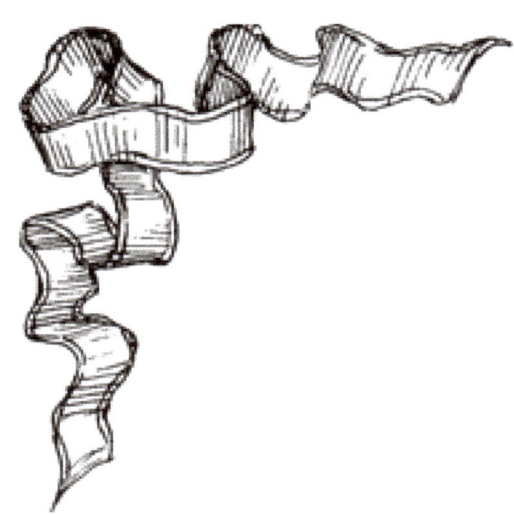

Are YOU Breathing?

Born in Mankato, MN Michael Ploog is an American storyboard and comic book artist, and a visual designer for films. In comics, Ploog is best known for his work on Marvel Comics' 1970s Man-Thing and The Monster of Frankenstein series, and as the initial artist on the features Ghost Rider and Werewolf by Night. His style at the time was heavily influenced by the art of Will Eisner, under whom he apprenticed. He's also done art for Hot Rod Cartoons, CARtoons and Cycletoons and for Dr. Pepper commercials.

For film, he's done storyboards, set design and other work for Wizards, Heavy Metal, Lord of the Rings, Dark Crystal, Superman II, Superman III, Supergirl, Ghostbusters, Good Morning Vietnam and Melvin and Howard among others. In 1990 Mike also painted an adaptation of "The Adventures of Tom Sawyer" for First's Classic Illustrated and did covers for First's Lone Wolf and Cub.

CPSIA information can be obtained
at www.ICGtesting.com
Printed in the USA
BVHW021054200922
647488BV00010B/310